Financial Planning 101

The Novice Investor's Guide Toward
Financial Independence

John & Joanne –
Thank you for your
confidence & trust through
the years!

CHIP GORDY

This piece is dedicated to my lovely wife and children, my exceptional parents, and my (little) brother who help me keep everything in perspective

Table of Contents

*An investment in knowledge pays
the best interest.*

˜˙ Benjamin Franklin

Why Financial Planning?

Financial planning is not solely for the wealthy. It's becoming evident that financial planning is even more important for the Individual with an average income than it is for someone who earns a very high income. Why? Because the average individual has to build their Income to cover many needs, and normally there's little cash left each month after paying all the bills and loans.

Therefore, financial planning can help you in a number of ways. Among them are:

Assisting you to set up favorable use of your present income and savings. By having every household's outlay budgeted and a savings outline put together, it should help you spend your cash sensibly and effectively.

It can help offset the effects of inflation on your money by having your savings invested in an investment vehicle that pays higher returns than the normal bank account, coupled with the correct amount of risk that you're willing to take.

It can direct you to take advantage of savings and investment options that exist now, but may not be available later. For example, you want to put some of your savings in a particular investment that pays a decent return, but the investment will only be available for a short period of time. If you had some extra money available and earmarked for this type of asset, you could take advantage of the opportunity.

By observing where you are financially at a certain point, you can see whether you're on track to meet your goals or not.

Finally, financial planning helps you identify the expected sources and total of your retirement income, while helping you project what future expenses you could expect as well.

By starting your retirement planning now, you can measure how much money you will require to maintain your current lifestyle and where it will come from. What you also get is a working plan that can be adjusted as time goes by. Remember: planning is a process that can change as you go through different stages and events in life.

Unfortunately, many individuals, specifically those who have just started working, put off their retirement planning for various reasons, usually because they think they're too young. The opposite is true because by starting early to save for retirement, you'll be able to save and put in more due to the concept of compounding interest (provided that you invest your savings wisely).

Let's face it: it's really difficult to keep track of your financial picture. If you have, at the very least, a flexible financial plan in place, it may help to direct you or get you close to where you'd like to be in the future.

The Dangers of No Financial Plan

It's a common misconception that it's always less expensive to do it yourself. In fact, entire industries have cropped up around this myth. Just drive around any area and look for major hardware supply stores in your area. These stores exist and succeed because we've been told we can save the expense of hiring contractors, carpenters, plumbers, and electricians by doing the job ourselves. But when you consider the price of the materials and the price of the tools you need to buy to do it right, and the time invested not only in the project but often in redoing the project when you realize you did it wrong the first time, is it really worth it?

Most big businesses don't think so. Instead of spending time and money learning to do a specific task themselves, or hiring someone full time, they've found it much more cost-effective to hire professional consultants. Today there appears to be a professional consultant for almost everything. There are management consultants, marketing consultants, business consultants, sales consultants, construction consultants, job or employment consultants, and the list goes on.

And if you stop and think, it makes sense. In today's fast-paced and changing world, there's just too much information you need to know, especially if you want to make good decisions. It's just really simple to make a bad decision based on limited or inadequate knowledge and experience. Most people should understand what big businesses already know: in the long run, doing it yourself can cost you much more than hiring a consultant or specialist.

This is especially true in the financial services industry. Very few people can invest enough time to learn everything they need to know about insurance and finance. And what appears to be very simple on the surface is very complicated when you know all the facts. That's one of the reasons why so many people are struggling financially today. They've made some very serious and costly mistakes, like choosing the wrong investments. Too many people have put all their savings at risk and have lost more and more of their money in recent years. Others are being too conservative and their investment growth is not even keeping pace with inflation. One of the biggest problems I see every day is how many people haven't positioned themselves correctly and are paying considerably more taxes than they should. Still others have bought the wrong types and amounts of insurance and they or their families are paying the consequences.

Following are some common investment mistakes that you want to keep in mind:

Trying to time the market. Nobody can time the market again and again. If they could, there would be people who have never lost money in the short term. It's a big mistake to think that people can win consistently, especially people who don't do it full time. It's important to understand that there's always someone else on the other side of a trade. So if one person wins in the short term, another person technically loses. For example, if you sell at a profit and the stock goes down, you win and the buyer loses. But if the stock continues to rise, you've lost the gain you could have had and the buyer wins by getting it. Professionals on Wall Street who do this for living have much better chances of winning. So for amateurs to think they can time the market and beat the professionals (and others) consistently, they're probably making a costly mistake.

Another misstep is **taking investment advice from friends**, families, or a rumor without doing the proper due diligence. Make it a high priority to have a disciplined approach to investing. Out of the tips that you got in the past, how many of them turned out to be right? There's no problem with getting advice from a non-professional, but it's important not to follow it blindly. If you get this type of an investment suggestion, see how it fits with your current investment plan. Being disciplined is vital because it's in our investment nature to buy high and sell low. Remember: by the time an investment tip rolls around, chances are the investment is already close to its top and the professional traders are ready to take a profit.

The last frequent error is **failing to pay attention to fees and costs**. I recently had someone come to me and after doing their research of their portfolio, realized they were paying 3 percent in fees every year in addition to the commission their broker was getting. This means that at a minimum, the fee brings down their portfolio 3 percent right from the start, and they need to earn 3 percent more than their target goal per year. So if a 7 percent annual return is needed to meet your financial goals, the portfolio needs to perform at 10 percent or more per year. If the market is even for an extended period of time, high fees can erode your portfolio's value. There is nothing wrong with paying someone to help you manage your finances, especially if you have no desire, time, or knowledge to do so. But pay attention to the fees and make sure the advisor has your best interests at heart. Remember, this is your money, and only you can make the best decision for it. You may not have time or expertise to manage your investments, so find someone that does and make sure the costs are sensible.

I highly recommend finding a professional consultant whom you can trust and rely on. You want someone who will take the time to help you understand all your options. Choosing the proper advisor or consultant is the key to having the financial freedom you have earned and deserve.

Analyzing Your Financial Picture

Before investing or making any financial decisions, you first need to analyze and understand your entire financial picture. A balance sheet and a cash flow statement enable you to take an in-depth look at your current financial situation and make better decisions about the future. With a little work, you can develop these two tools and be on your way to a solid plan for your finances.

A **balance sheet** is a snapshot of your personal finances at one point in time. It contains two main parts: what you own (assets), and what you owe (liabilities). Your net worth (or equity) is simply your assets minus your liabilities.

Examples of assets include your house, investments (stocks, bonds, real estate), savings and checking accounts, 401(k), IRAs, business interests, artwork, and jewelry, among others. Liabilities include mortgage balances, credit cards, education loans, and any other debt.

The ultimate goal of most investors is to increase their net worth. The balance sheet is a very useful tool to identify strengths and weaknesses in your current finances, as well as to determine your goals for the future. Someone with a high amount of liability might set a goal to eliminate this debt. On the other hand, someone with a positive net worth (more assets than liabilities) might plan to save and invest towards retirement, college, or another goal.

After examining your balance sheet and determining your goals, you need to decide how to fund these goals. A well-formulated plan is one not only with realistic goals, but also a sensible means of achieving them. In other words, having goals is good, but you must be able to pay for them. Using a cash flow statement will help you to determine how to pay for your goals.

A **cash flow statement** is a detailed look at all money coming in and going out over a period of time. It shows what you earn (income) and what you spend (expenses). Your net cash flow is what you earn minus what you spend.

Some examples of income include salary and wages, self-employment earnings, dividends, interest, and other investment income. Expenses may include mortgage payments, rent payments, insurance costs, utilities, clothing, food, child care, alimony or child support, travel, entertainment, loan payments, education costs, taxes, charitable contributions, gifts, and gasoline.

By analyzing your cash flow statement, you can more easily cut expenses and identify excess net cash to use towards your goals. Generally, someone with negative net cash flow should first concentrate on cutting expenses to achieve positive cash flow before attempting to save or invest towards any future goals. Once positive net cash flow is attained, excess money can be used for funding and achieving your goals.

When using these two tools, it's important to remember the more detail you use, the more effective they will be. A plan is only as good as the effort you put forth when creating it.

Creating a Financial Plan

The investment policy statement (a written investment plan) is a very important factor of successful investing. This allows you to have a written review program for managing your investments. It also provides a means for measuring results.

It outlines an investor's circumstances, including their objectives and limits, risk tolerance, return objectives, liquidity needs, time horizon, and the investment tactics to be used. It's a written roadmap to help you steer through the future to reach your investment objectives.

This policy statement helps you stay disciplined even when market movements are difficult and your emotions may be causing you to second-guess your strategy. It also promotes communication with others involved. It forms an outline for reviewing important factors as they change over time.

Following are the steps to forming an investment policy statement:

Establish your long-term goals. Some of your objectives may include the need for supplemental retirement income in order to sustain your quality of life through retirement, educational funding, or the purchase of a vacation home. Just remember to account for future inflation potential and the need to make sufficient income.

Define your investment time horizon. You could have more than one investment objective, each with a different investment period, so make sure all are identified in your policy statement. Your time horizon is important because it will affect your asset matter allocation and risk profile and how your investments might change over time.

Establish your risk profile. Markets can be and usually are volatile, so it's important to establish an acceptable and appropriate amount of risk for your situation. There are many different ways to calculate risk, including trying to calculate the chance that your expected returns may be less than expected. A financial advisor can help you with this.

Establish an expected rate of return. To reach your financial goal, your portfolio will need to increase in value at a certain rate. You want to take this into account and work this into your investment plan. You need to determine criteria for regular appraisal of your results compared to benchmarks and expectations.

Form your asset combination. This will assist you in the continuing management of your assets. Your portfolio's asset classes should have a low correlation to provide diversification. Other matters include liquidity, rebalancing rules, and tax efficiency.

Document an investment strategy. There are many ways you can execute an investment program. Be sure to carefully evaluate different tactics and record your choices in your policy statement. This will help guide you as market conditions change, and you might think about new investment classes and tactics in the future.

Tips on Wise Investing

One of the most common requests I receive is for investing help. Besides having a plan there are just a few basic investing tips to remember when you plan for your future through investing.

Diversify your investments. Create a balanced portfolio to help you stay on track and reach your goals. Why? Well, for one thing, while the entire stock market may be here for the rest of your life, any one stock might not be. Remember to heed the old adage "Don't put all of your eggs in one basket."

Obviously, if you're invested in many asset classes (stocks, bonds, cd's, etc.) as opposed to one, then you may minimize your risk accordingly.

Just about every investment has some type of risk connected with it. The stock market goes up and goes down. A rise in interest rates can cause a fall in the bond market. What about real estate? Too much supply and not enough demand can affect even your most important investment – your primary home. No matter what you decide to invest your money in, risk is something you must think about, and proper diversification can help minimize this risk.

A simple example of diversification goes like this.

At a particular resort, the entire economy consists of two companies: one that sells umbrellas and another that sells sunscreen. If a portfolio is completely invested in the company that sells umbrellas, it will have strong performance during the rainy season, but poor performance when the weather is sunny. The opposite happens if the portfolio is only invested in the sunscreen company, the alternative investment: the portfolio will have a better performance when the sun is out, but will go down when it's cloudy. To minimize the weather-dependent risk in this portfolio, the investment should be split between the companies. With this diversified portfolio, returns should be good no matter what the weather conditions are, rather than alternating between sunny and rainy.

One of the keys to being a successful investor is managing risk while having the potential for sufficient return on your investments. One of the most effective ways to help manage your investment risk is to diversify. Like the example above, diversification is an investment strategy aimed at managing risk by spreading your money across a variety of investments such as stocks, bonds, real estate, and cash alternatives.

Similarly, the power of diversification may help smooth the bumpy ride that just about every portfolio can have over time. As one investment increases, it may offset the decreases in another. This may allow your portfolio to ride out market ebbs and flows, while providing a steadier performance under various economic conditions. By reducing the impact of market ups and downs, diversification can go far in improving your comfort level with investing.

Diversification is one of the main reasons why professionally managed portfolios are so attractive for both experienced and novice investors. Many non-institutional investors have a limited investment budget and may find it a challenge to construct a portfolio that's well-enough diversified, let alone have the time to actually monitor it.

Using a small initial investment, you can purchase shares in a diversified portfolio of stocks, bonds, REITs (Real Estate Investment Trusts), or many other investment vehicles, depending on the objectives of the fund. You also (usually) get expert investment selection in the portfolio.

Whether you're Investing in mutual funds or are putting together your own combination of stocks, bonds, and other investment instruments, it's a good idea to keep in mind the importance of this concept. Diversification does not eliminate or guarantee against the risk of investment loss; it's a method used to help manage investment risk. The value of stocks, bonds, and mutual funds always fluctuates with market conditions. But diversification, when used correctly, can help protect your investments from fluctuating too much.

Beware of get rich quick schemes. If an investment seems too good to be true, it probably is. Usually the higher the estimated return, the higher the risk to you. "No guts, no glory" works better on a ski slope than when you're investing. Stick with time-proven ways to grow your investments.

One time-proven method is called dollar-cost averaging. When using this plan, you're investing a certain fixed amount at the same interval (i.e., $200 every 15th of the month). This will allow you to "automatically" buy a security at different values over a certain time frame with the intention that over time the value of what you're buying will go up. Most people don't realize this, but they're performing this strategy when investing in their employer's retirement plan.

Feel comfortable with your investment decisions. If the risk in your investments keeps you from sleeping at night, then you're taking too much risk. It's always a good idea to profile your investment type through a risk questionnaire that your investment advisor can provide. Re-evaluate your investment plan periodically and as life changes occur.

Keep good records and check your statements each time you receive them. Always question anything that doesn't look right or that you don't understand. For instance, you should understand all applicable investment charges and fees up front.

Seek guidance. Investing, if done properly, can be a foundation to your future wealth. So don't forget to follow these tips when you invest and, as always, seek the guidance from an investment professional.

Make Savings a Priority

You've heard the expression, pay yourself first. It's important to include savings in your budget and not wait until you have money left over after all of the expenses are paid. Your savings will grow faster if you make them a priority. Here are some different ways to contribute to your savings to put you in the best financial situation.

Save for Emergencies

Financial emergencies have become much more common recently. While we can't predict exactly what kind of financial emergency may happen each year, they do happen. Not having a savings fund for emergencies can be very costly and very exasperating.

"Downsizing" has been common over the past few years, and many of the people who have been laid off are unprepared for such an emergency because they have high levels of personal debt and little or no savings. Even if you receive severance pay, you may need to use some of your savings for times when you don't have an income. The rule of thumb for the amount of your emergency savings should be at least six months' worth of expenses.

Save for Retirement

Another common rule of thumb in developing a retirement savings strategy is that your accumulated savings and other sources of income will need to replace about 80 percent of your pre-retirement income.

You can maintain your standard of living with less income because your taxes could be lower, there would be no need for retirement salary deferrals, your mortgage(s) may be paid off before or soon after you retire, and you would no longer have work-related expenses such as commuting and business clothing.

Although an 80 percent income replacement ratio is a reasonable goal, it doesn't indicate how much you need to accumulate and what to expect from other income sources. That could depend on several of the following factors.

Career earnings. If you have had high earnings over your career, Social Security may replace a lower proportion of your pre-retirement income. For instance, a 65-year-old who retired with a lifetime of high annual earnings (equivalent to roughly $68,800) could expect Social Security to replace merely 34 percent of his pre-retirement salary.

Rates of return. Higher investment returns might result in a higher income stream, but this also involves a higher degree of risk. Rates of return will vary over time, so it might be a good idea to use a moderate return rate for your long-term projections.

Age when you begin saving. The earlier you start, the less you may need to save out of each paycheck because compounding should enhance your overall savings accumulation.

Age of retirement. The earlier you retire, the less time you may have to accumulate savings and the longer your retirement might last. This generally means that you will need to increase your savings rate while you are working.

Another approach is to think in terms of saving a multiple of your final pre-retirement salary. One analysis that factored in inflation and post-retirement medical costs suggested that employees would need to accumulate assets equal to 11 times their final salaries to meet their retirement needs (beyond the income they would receive from Social Security).

However, another recent study of more than 2 million employees discovered that workers who saved for retirement throughout their careers were on track to accumulate 8.8 times their final salaries (on average), resulting in a shortfall of 2.2 times salary. Yet the same study found that if workers increased their contributions by 1 percent of salary each year for five years, the number of people who could retire with sufficient assets would increase from 29 percent to 46 percent. For someone earning $70,000 annually, a 1 percent increase equates to saving less than $3 each workday.

Of course, the amount you need to save for retirement will also depend on other variables such as your lifestyle, your post-retirement medical expenses, the length of your retirement, and your supplementary sources of income. The key is to develop a solid strategy and maintain a steady pace toward your savings goal.

Contribute to Employer-Sponsored Retirement Plans

One out of every four Americans today is not taking advantage of the best savings and investment option available partly because they fear they will not be able to access their money. In 2016, some of the most common employer-sponsored plans allow you to save up to $18,000 ($24,000 if you are 50 or older) per year from your gross income, tax deductible. In addition, your employer can contribute or match a certain amount to your 401(k) or 403(b) plans. If you don't have a plan at work, you can still contribute up to $5,500 annually to an IRA ($6,500 if you are 50 or older), which can also be fully deductible in certain instances.

Other Goal-Based Savings

Many parents and future students see college as the connection between this life and a better one. As more high-school graduates are going to college, many are under pressure with how they're going to pay for it.

We get many questions about what types of accounts are offered to help save for college. Here are a few.

UGMA/UTMA Accounts. These are a college savings option that can also provide tax-free savings without higher expenses associated with maintaining other plans, while also having a significant amount of control over the types of investments made during accumulation. The account-holder can also have more control during the distribution phase when the money is taken out. Finally, there is some flexibility because the money doesn't have to be used for college, so should the beneficiary decide not to go to college, the money could be used elsewhere.

College Savings Plans. The benefit of these is that they grow tax deferred, and withdrawals to pay for college expenses aren't taxed.

There are two kinds of college savings plans: pre-paid and savings. Pre-paid plans usually allow a lump sum up front, "pre-paying" all or part of the cost of an in-state public college education now, at a lower amount. The last time I checked, the college tuition inflation rate was over 7 percent per year, so you're securing future college costs. They can also be converted for use at private and out-of-state colleges.

The other type, a savings plan, allows you to make regular deposits, which also grow tax-deferred. One of the main differences with this type of plan is that is similar to investing in an investment portfolio, and volatility may affect the account value, whereas with a pre-paid plan you really don't see any fluctuations.

So which type of plan works best? That depends on if you can afford to pre-pay all at once, or if you'd rather make deposits along the way. There are also no real guarantees with the savings account as the value could potentially dwindle to nothing.

U.S. Savings Bonds. EE and I bonds purchased after 1989 by someone at least 24 years old can be redeemed tax-free when the bond owners or dependents pay for college tuition and fees. There is usually a tax exclusion phase-out for incomes between certain levels, and they sometimes change year-to-year.

Coverdell Education Savings Accounts. Earnings grow tax-deferred and distributions are tax-free when used for qualified post-secondary education costs.

The choice of which type of account to use to fund college expenses can be cumbersome, so make sure to get professional advice to help you decide why type works best for your situation.

Why Invest Early?

Compound interest is vital to your investment growth. Whether your financial portfolio consists of just a deposit account at your local bank, stocks, bonds, or a series of highly-leveraged investments, your rate of return is considerably improved by the compounding factor.

With compound interest, the return that you receive on your initial investment is automatically reinvested. In other words, you're making interest on the interest. But just how quickly does your money grow? Or to be more specific, how long will it take to double?

I could write out the formula for this equation, but the easiest way to work that out is by using what's known as the Rule of 72. Simply put, the Rule of 72 enables you to figure out how long it will take for the money that you've invested on a compound interest basis to double. You divide 72 by the interest rate to get the answer.

For example, if you invest $5,000 at 10 percent compound interest, then the Rule of 72 states that in 7.2 years you will have $10,000. You divide 72 by 10 percent to get the time it takes for your money to double. The Rule of 72 is a generally reliable method that gives approximate results. It's most accurate for hypothetical rates between 5 and 20 percent.

One of the important steps to take when in making an investment decision is working out the real rate of return on your investment (nominal interest less inflation). Consequently, while compound interest is a big friend to an investor, inflation is one of our greatest enemies. The Rule of 72 can also highlight the potential damage that inflation can do to your money.

Let's say you decide not to invest your $5,000 but hide it in a shoebox under your bed instead, and then forget it's there. Assuming an inflation rate of 4.5 percent, in 16 years your $5,000 will have lost half of its value (or purchasing power) due to the erosive effect of price increases.

The real rate of return is the key to how quickly the value of your investment will grow. If you're receiving 10 percent interest on an investment, but inflation is running at 4 percent, then your real rate of return is only 6 percent. In such a scenario, it will take your money 12 years to double in value.

The Rule of 72 is a quick and easy way to determine the value of compound interest over time. By taking the real rate of return into consideration, you can see, in general terms, how soon a particular investment will double in value. By starting early, you put yourself in the best possible position to maximize your portfolio growth.

Put Your Financial House in Order

In addition to making wise savings decisions, there are several things you can do to put yourself in the best financial position.

Create a budget

Making and sticking to a budget doesn't have to be as hard as most people think. All you have to do is follow these easy steps.

Gather every financial statement and bill that you can. This means everything that you have that shows what you have coming in, and what you have going out. The key here is to establish a monthly average, and the more information you can get to, the better.

Record all of your sources of income. If you're self-employed or have any other sources of earnings, be sure to record these too. If your income is in the form of a regular paycheck where taxes are automatically deducted, then use the take-home amount. Calculate this total income as a monthly amount.

Create a list of monthly expenses. Write down a list of all the expenses you plan on having over the course of a month, including your mortgage, car payments, auto insurance, groceries, utilities, entertainment, retirement or college savings, and everything else you spend money on. Make this your monthly amount.

Break expenses into two categories: static and variable. Static expenses are those that stay fairly the same each month and are necessary parts of your way of living. They include your mortgage or rent, car payments, utilities, credit card payments, and so on. These expenses, for the most part, are necessary yet not likely to change in the budget. Variable expenses are the type that will change from month to month, and include items such as groceries, gasoline, and entertainment, to name a few. This category will be important when making changes.

Total your monthly income and monthly expenses. If your end result shows more income than expenses, you're off to a good start. This means you can allot this excess to areas such as savings or paying more on credit cards. If you have more expenses than income, it means some modifications need to be made.

Make adjustments to expenses if necessary. If you have recognized and listed all of your expenses, the objective would be to have your income and expense columns to be equal. This means all of your income is accounted for and budgeted for a specific expense. If you are in a situation where expenses are higher than income, you should look at your variable expenses to find areas to curtail.

Pay off your debts as quickly as possible

People today carry an average balance of nearly $5000 or more on their credit cards during the year. By paying off your credit cards, you're saving (or earning, depending on how you look at it) the equivalent of up to 25 to 28 percent interest on your money. Once that debt has been paid, the monthly credit payment can then be reapplied to paying off your mortgage or saving for retirement.

Furthermore, in the event of a job loss or other financial emergency, you avoid the prospect of having creditors and debt-collection agencies pestering you for payment. As you pay off each debt, apply the payment for that debt toward your other debts to pay them off much faster.

Pay off your mortgage early

Not only can this become a key means of saving for retirement, but money saved in this way is flexible. With a home equity loan, you can deal with a financial emergency or help pay for a child's college education. Also, if you become unemployed, your mortgage holder may be more willing to make temporary adjustments or other concessions in your monthly mortgage payment if you have been prepaying on your mortgage.

Money saved by paying off your mortgage early will not only save you a bundle in the long run, but it's similar to earning tax-free interest. For example, prepaying a 7 percent mortgage is like earning 7 percent interest tax free because the interest doesn't accrue as much over time.

Some people prefer to make a small additional payment with each monthly mortgage payment. Others prefer to make additional payments yearly and use any windfall or extra income for this purpose. Either way, you should talk to your bank or lender and see if they will allow pre-payments. And of course, make sure that you're not sacrificing any of your other obligations.

Manage your estate planning

Keep records in a system that others can understand and access. Should something happen to you, it will be easier to sort out your affairs. Both partners in a marriage or long-term relationship should know where all financial and legal records are, as well as the names of lawyers, accountants, and other advisers. Make a will and review it periodically to ensure it continues to reflect your wishes.

Manage your taxes

Consult with experts well before April 1 each year. Keep good records. A business diary is one way to track deductible expenses. If you use credit cards for business travel and expenses, note the nature of the expense on the back of the slip you keep. Remember, every dollar you save in taxes equals an extra dollar in income.

Maintain a high credit score

When you submit an application for credit, the creditor usually requires your credit report. This report is a compilation of both your credit score and your current and past payment history. The score is based on you as a credit risk and many other issues, like your income, length of employment, and years you've lived in your home.

Your credit score can vary anywhere from 300 to 850, as the higher the score the lower the level of implied credit risk. A score of 620 or better is usually deemed creditworthy, and a score of 670 and higher is considered excellent. Typically, scores of 720 and above receive the best deals on interest rates, as the higher the credit score, the lower the interest rate usually is. The most important issues that influence your credit score are as follows.

Promptness of bill payments. This is a no brainer, but it's always good to check your credit report to see if there are any late notices. This is also the largest component of your score, consisting of 35 percent of the total. Lenders like to see that you've paid all your bills on time for at least the past seven years.

Credit inquiries. Roughly 10 percent of your score is related to the number of credit inquiries by lenders in the last six months.

Outstanding debt. Accounting for 30 percent of your score, this is a gauge of your "credit utilization ratio": how much of your available credit is remaining.

Credit history. This shows how long your credit history is with different lenders and relates to 15 percent of your current score.

Debt mix. The final 10 percent of your score is based on whether you've made payments on time for other of types of debt like a mortgage, car loans, or credit cards.

Here are some other things that you can do to help improve your score no matter where you fall on the credit-rating scale.

Don't discontinue every credit card that you don't use. This has the result of increasing your credit utilization ratio because you have less available credit. On the other hand, if you have too many open credit cards (say, more than five), consider closing either the newer ones or the ones with lower limits.

Curtail requests for more credit. Inquiries regarding additional debt show up in your credit file and have the potential to reduce your credit score.

Reduce your credit utilization ratio. You have a higher score when your outstanding debt as a percentage of your available debt is lower. A good rule of thumb is to have your credit utilization never go over 50 percent (meaning don't use more than half of your available credit).

Get a copy of your credit report at least every three months to make sure your information is correct.

Manage Your Risk

When you start to create or recreate your own personal financial plan, or even some type of risk-management scheme, there are some ways that you can manage your day-to-day risks. It should be first pointed out that some techniques are required by law, like car or flood insurance. Nevertheless, not all risks are as controllable or as apparent as a flooded garage.

When gauging the perils in terms of your financial well-being, we're each responsible to a certain extent to make the decision on how we'll manage them. Following are three common methods to manage risk.

Risk Transfer. A very popular risk-management technique is risk transfer. Transferring risk from one party to another helps reduce a possible liability or other financial damage when engaging In an activity that exposes you to a potential loss.

There are two major ways transfer risk: insurance and non-insurance. Risk transfer through insurance is also referred to as one of the methods of financing or "outsourcing" your risk management. By purchasing insurance, you're actually transferring the financial risk of potential losses to an insurance company.

Non-insurance transfers can also occur through legally binding contracts, such as insurance. However, you can also decide to transfer risk to another party through the use of services and subcontracting. The use of third parties through contracts will put the financial liability of damages on them, relieving you of the risk and any subsequent loss.

Risk Avoidance. Avoiding a particular risk completely will eliminate any probability of loss from the event. Choosing to completely avoid a risk is only possible for a few hazards of everyday life. Deciding not to put a trampoline in your backyard will help avoid the risk of someone getting injured. However, you can't completely avoid the risk of storm damage to your primary home or property because you have very little control over the weather.

Risk Retention. The last of the common risk-management techniques is the retaining the risk. This technique is almost the opposite of risk avoidance. When you make the decision to not avoid or transfer the risk, you're essentially financing the risk yourself. All losses that happen through this method of managing a risk threat will be paid by you.

Businesses that have an enough of a capital cushion oftentimes decide to retain some risks rather than buying insurance to cover any potential losses if they've done their homework and can determine that the risk vs. reward is positive. Many individuals also sometimes decide to retain some risk through the use of a high-deductible insurance policy.

Safeguarding your financial future starts with some degree of financial planning and suitable risk management.

Homeowner's Insurance

Make a household inventory. In the event of fire or loss, you will need it to document insurance claims. Once a year, review the primary and secondary beneficiaries on your policies and evaluate contracts of all your homeowner's or renter's, car, and other personal property insurance.

Health Insurance

Health insurance, now required by law, is an important part of managing risk. According to a study by NerdWallet Health, health-related expenses are the number one cause of personal bankruptcy in the United States. Find the proper insurance to cover you and your family and plan for additional medical expenses not covered by insurance, like co-pays, prescriptions, and dental coverage. It's important to choose your coverage carefully to meet your current needs and any unexpected injuries and illnesses to avoid dipping into emergency or retirement savings to pay the additional expenses.

As with any type of insurance, it's always recommended to speak with a professional to help you decide what form of health insurance will work best for your unique situation.

Life Insurance

We've all heard about how important it is to have life insurance, but is it really necessary? Usually the answer is "yes," but it depends on your specific situation. If you have a family who relies on your income, then it's very important to have life insurance protection. If you're single and have no major assets to protect, then you may not need coverage.

In the event of your premature death, your beneficiaries can use funds from a life insurance policy to replace many different types of expenses, including funeral and burial expenses, probate, estate taxes, day care, and any number of everyday expenses. Funds can be used to pay for your children's education and take care of debts or a mortgage that hasn't been paid off. Life insurance funds can also be added to your spouse's retirement savings.

If your dependents will not require the proceeds from a life insurance policy for these types of expenses, you may wish to name a favorite charity as the beneficiary of your policy. Your estate could potentially get a tax benefit for your bequest, as well.

Whole life insurance can also be used as a source of cash in the event you need to access the funds during your lifetime. Many types of permanent life insurance build cash value that can be borrowed from or withdrawn at the policy owner's request. Of course, withdrawals or loans that are not repaid will reduce the policy's cash value and death benefit.

When considering what type of insurance to purchase and how much you need, ask yourself what would happen to your family without you and what type of legacy you would like to leave behind. Do you want to ensure that the funds will be sufficient to pay off the mortgage as well as achieve other goals? Do you want to ensure that your children's college expenses will be taken care of in your demise? Would you like to leave a sizable donation to your favorite charity? Life insurance may be able to help you meet your intentions and give you the confidence that your family will be taken care of financially.

The cost and availability of life insurance depend on factors such as age, health, and the type and amount of insurance purchased. As with most financial decisions, there are expenses associated with the purchase of life insurance. Policies commonly have mortality and expense charges. In addition, if a policy is surrendered prematurely, there may be surrender charges and income tax implications. Any guarantees are contingent on the claims-paying ability of the issuing insurance company.

If you're considering the purchase of life insurance, always consult a financial and/or legal professional to help explore your options.

Longevity Insurance

The number of Americans aged 90 and older almost tripled between 1980 and 2010, and is expected to quadruple by 2050. Life expectancies represent the average number of years someone of a certain age is expected to live, so you might live longer.

Even though a longer life span is a positive trend, many people may find it challenging to make their savings last throughout a long retirement.

If you'd like a steady income that could last throughout retirement, you might consider purchasing longevity insurance, a fixed annuity that provides a guaranteed monthly income starting sometime in the future. An annuity purchased today might begin providing a steady income stream in 10, 20, or 30 years (depending on the contract), and could continue for as long as you live.

Because the annuity is deferred, premiums would typically be lower than they would be with an immediate annuity. And the longer the annuity is deferred, the higher the monthly income could be.

Without a source of guaranteed income, it might be difficult to estimate how much to withdraw each month from your retirement savings. Withdraw too much, and you risk running out of money in your lifetime. Withdraw too little, and you may live on a more limited budget than necessary, missing out on some of the experiences you looked forward to enjoying in retirement.

Longevity insurance might help you feel more comfortable making withdrawals during the earlier phase of retirement, knowing that a guaranteed income stream would be available when you reach a specific age. For example, a 65-year-old who purchases longevity insurance that would begin at age 80 might draw down more retirement assets over the 15-year period before the annuity income starts than he or she would have been able to do otherwise.

Annuity payouts could also be structured to continue throughout the lifetime of a second individual, providing income for a surviving spouse for as long as the contract remains in force. This may be especially important for women, who often are younger than their spouses and typically live longer than men.

Premiums for a fixed annuity can be paid in a lump sum or a series of payments. If the insured dies before annuity payouts begin, the insurer will generally keep the premiums that were paid. You should be aware that funds invested in a fixed annuity do not have the opportunity to pursue potentially higher returns in the financial markets. And inflation could reduce the future purchasing power of the annuity payouts.

A fixed annuity is an insurance-based contract. Any guarantees are contingent on the claims-paying ability of the issuing insurance company. Generally, annuities have contract limitations, fees, and expenses. Most annuities have surrender charges that are assessed during the early years of the contract. Withdrawals of annuity earnings are taxed as ordinary income. Early withdrawals prior to age 59½ may be subject to a 10 percent federal income-tax penalty.

Disability Insurance

Disability insurance, like life insurance, is used to protect future earnings. Disability insurance will replace your income in the event that you become physically unable to work. Although it gets less attention than life insurance, experts agree that disability coverage is at least as important.

While most people are prepared for the medical costs of severe injury or sickness (through health insurance), without disability insurance, they are not prepared for the loss of wages that accompanies such a tragedy.

In general, if you count on your job to pay the rent and buy food, you should seriously consider disability coverage.

Disability Insurance Policies

Many employers offer disability insurance for their employees; however, the plans vary greatly, and some may not offer adequate coverage. Furthermore, any disability payouts from an employer's policy are subject to taxes, while payouts from individual policies are not. Individual disability coverage is generally much more expensive than employer disability coverage; nevertheless, you should review any policies your employer has taken out, and consider purchasing individual coverage if the policy is insufficient.

Disability insurance comes in two types: short-term and long-term.

Short-term disability. This coverage replaces a portion of lost salary in the event the policy owner misses six months or less of work. The coverage typically begins after all sick leave is exhausted, and replaces close to 100 percent of wages for the first payouts. If the policy owner remains unable to work, however, the payments will eventually drop, often to 60 percent of wages. The length of coverage and payment percentage vary from plan to plan, but these numbers are typical.

Long-term disability. Some experts contend that long-term disability insurance is the most important insurance you can purchase. This can be partially attributed to advances in medical care; some diseases and injuries are now disabling rather than deadly, meaning that the incapacitation can be lengthy.

Typically, long-term disability insurance can be purchased to replace 50 to 70 percent of salary. Some employers allow employees to purchase extra insurance from the same company, sometimes raising the total to 80 percent. Note, however, that some policies have monthly maximum payouts, which may reduce the actual percentage of salary the policy owner receives. The "salary" is set at the time the policy is purchased, and you will likely want to increase the value of the plan as your compensation increases. Some plans only allow increases with a physical exam, some allow increases without a physical for the first few years of the plan, and some have other rules; check the plan for its particulars.

Long-term disability policies vary in the length of payout: some policies will only pay out for five or 10 years, and some will pay out until age 65. Experts recommend the latter. Policies also vary in definition of disability (some contentious categories include mental illness and back injuries) and exclusionary criteria (pre-existing medical conditions, injuries from dangerous activities, etc.).

Policies can be "guaranteed renewable" and "non-cancelable."

Guaranteed renewable means the insurance company cannot drop the policy unless premium payments are skipped.

Non-cancelable means the insurance company can never raise the premium on the policy.

Both are desirable, but non-cancelable is usually best.

There are a few important policy options (or "riders") that should be considered: "residual benefits" and "cost of living" (COLA).

The **residual benefits rider** provides the difference between old and new salaries in the event that the policy owner can get a new job, but not one with the same salary as his old one.

The **cost of living rider** allows the policy's value to increase with inflation.

Finally, a disability policy can be designated as an "own-occupation" policy. Most policies are "any-occupation," which means the policy owner must work when he is capable, even if not in the same capacity as before. An "own-occupation" policy will allow the owner to collect benefits until he can resume the previous occupation. Typically, these policies are more beneficial to policy-owners with high-skill or high-paying jobs.

Long-Term Care Insurance

Spending a long time in a nursing home or under home care is not something people like to think about; nevertheless, as medical science increases the average life expectancy, a growing number of seniors are finding themselves unable to live independently. At the same time, extended nursing home and home health care is becoming extremely expensive, primarily due to rising medical costs. Long-term care insurance covers these expenses, and is something people in their late 50s to 60s should seriously consider purchasing.

Long-term care policies generally cover extended health care at home, nursing homes, or assisted-living facilities. However, policies do not necessarily pay out in the same amounts for each of these choices; most notably, policies tend to pay less for home care. Like long-term disability coverage, policies also vary in their eligibility criteria, or the determination of when someone can no longer live independently. Experts say an ideal plan's eligibility criteria includes cognitive impairment and inability to perform one or more activities of daily living, and does not require previous hospitalization or home care.

Policies vary in their length of payout, from a couple of years to lifetime. Obviously, a lifetime policy charges higher premiums, but not much higher - the typical nursing homestay lasts less than three years, meaning the risk of a lifetime policy to the insurer is not that much greater than a two- or three-year policy.

Policies have a set amount of time between when care starts and when the benefits take effect, analogous to a deductible in other types of insurance coverage. The longer the waiting period is, the lower the premiums.

Finally, like long-term disability, long-term care policies can be "guaranteed renewable," meaning the insurance company cannot drop the policy. Most experts recommend a policy that's guaranteed renewable.

Protect Your Information

In light of recent events with some major retailers, here are some ways to help protect your identity from theft.

Use different passwords. Identity thieves love passwords because they open doors to our personal information. If possible, use different passwords each of your accounts, and make those passwords strong with at least eight characters, including a mix of letters and numbers. Hide them safely and keep them accessible. This may take some extra work, but fixing an identity theft problem is tougher.

Protect your Social Security number. Never carry your card with you, or any other card that may have your number (like an insurance card). Also, don't put the number on your checks. It's a major target for identity thieves because it gives them access to your credit report and bank accounts.

Always monitor your credit report! Get and carefully review your credit report at least once a year to check for suspicious activity. If you find something, alert your card company or the creditor immediately. You may also look into credit protection services, which alert you any time a change takes place with your credit report.

Destroy private records and statements. Tear up or shred credit card statements, solicitations, and other documents that contain private financial information.

Secure your mail. Empty your mailbox quickly, lock it, or get a post office box so no one will have a chance to steal any credit card offers you may receive. Also, don't mail outgoing bill payments and checks from home. They can be stolen from your mailbox and the payee's name erased with solvents. Mail them from the post office or another secure location.

Don't leave a paper trail. Never leave ATM, credit card, or gas station receipts behind.

Never let your credit card out of your sight. Worried about credit card skimming? Always keep an eye on your card or, when that's not possible, pay with cash.

Know who you're dealing with. Whenever anyone contacts you asking for private identity or financial information, make no response other than to find out who they are, what company they represent, and the reason for the call. If you think the request is legitimate, contact the company yourself and confirm what you were told before revealing any of your personal data.

Take your name off telemarketers' lists. In addition to the national Do-Not-Call registry, you can also cut down on junk mail and opt out of credit card solicitations.

Be more defensive with personal information. Ask salespeople and others if information such as Social Security or driver's license number is absolutely necessary. Ask anyone who does require your Social Security number about their privacy policy and make it clear that you do not want your information given to anyone else.

Review your credit-card statements carefully. Make sure you recognize the merchants, locations, and purchases listed before paying the bill. If you don't need or use department-store or bank-issued credit cards, consider closing the accounts.

Bank securely online. Online banking is growing at a very fast rate - so much so that virtually every bank is offering online banking to its customers. There are big advantages for the banks because the transactions and therefore the work is done by the customers themselves, and customers can access their online bank account 24/7. The following are some good ideas if you do your banking online.

Never use a password which is easily recognizable. Your password choice and its security are vital. Your password is your access to your online banking account. If your first name is "George," then it's advisable for you not to use your first name as your password on your account, nor any combination that contains your name. Also, you shouldn't use the same password for several accounts. By doing this, you reduce the risk of your password information falling into the wrong hands.

Recording your password. If you need to write down your password(s), make sure you put them in a secure place. For instance, having your password information in your wallet isn't advisable because you could possibly lose your wallet or it may be stolen.

Sending password information to others online. Never give your password details to anyone online, as information which is passed to others over the internet remains on the internet forever. Someone somewhere will have a copy of your previously-sent information, and that fact makes your password information unsecure and less safe. This may sound like a no-brainer, but it's happened in the past.

Have anti-spyware software installed on your computer. Spyware programs can be downloaded or installed and end up on your computer. An innocent request for information about a product can result in a spyware program going straight to your hard drive. Its function is to monitor computer usage activity and then communicate that information to its owner. Its function was originally set up to collect marketing information. But hackers can also use it to collect sensitive and secure information like your password and account information in relation to an online banking transaction. Therefore, having an anti-spyware program will protect you against a third party collecting information about your online banking activities.

Update your security and anti-virus software regularly. You can do this by ensuring that your computer security software is set up to update regularly when updates become available. This is very important because security patches are released primarily to fix a security issue or weakness. Installing the patch as soon as it becomes available will help you protect your online banking account information.

Financial Resolutions

As part of your planning for the year, consider taking action to better your personal finances. To get started, here are some goals and how to achieve them.

Stick to a budget. You should know exactly where your money's going and where you might make improvements. I've written about this before, and once you get started it's not too difficult. What's not so simple for some? Following through! If you want to break out of the cycle of living paycheck-to-paycheck and learn how to spend within your means, keeping a budget is a smart first step.

Pay off debt. There are many strategies out there to help you cut away your debt. You can start by paying down the debt that has the highest interest rate first and then work your way down. Just make sure you're still making at least the minimum payments on your other credit cards and loans.

Manage your credit. Your credit is more important than ever; it's absolutely vital to getting the best interest rates and terms for credit cards, home loans, and auto loans. If you have poor credit, you may not be able to qualify for credit at all in this economic environment.

The first step to managing your credit is to check your credit report at least every three months to make sure what's there is accurate. Staying on top of your credit doesn't have to cost you anything. Many credit companies will give you a free credit report.

Pay yourself first. This simply means that you need to save before you spend. A good way to do this is by setting up direct deposit from your paycheck into a savings account. This accomplishes two things. First, your deposit is automatic and it's almost like paying a monthly bill. Second, your deposit will hopefully go into an interest-bearing account or savings vehicle, and you'll be less likely to spend it.

Save more. Assume you're depositing $250 per paycheck toward your savings. Maybe you could find a way to increase your savings contribution to $350 per paycheck. Look for possible ways to cut unnecessary expenses. If you need a big-ticket item, do your research and look for sales. You can find ways to save more if you look for them.

Save for retirement. Here's another case where direct deposit makes it easy and effortless to save for your future. And if you're lucky enough to work for a company that matches your retirement contribution, take advantage of it! If you don't, you're essentially losing free money.

Get the proper insurance. If you have children, life insurance is, of course, imperative. A good rule of thumb is to have a policy with a benefit of seven to 10 times your annual household income.

Finally, when you need help, turn to a professional. When seeking out a financial advisor, work with someone you trust and who understands you and your financial objectives. A financial advisor knows the markets and tools to help you achieve your goals, even as your goals may change over time. As a captain and a sounding board on your financial team, they offer you confidence during the good times and the challenging ones and take the worry out of making financial decisions for tomorrow and today.

Financial Terms

Here are some commonly-used terms in the financial world.

Bull: An optimistic investor who thinks the market or a specific security or an industry will rise.

Bear: A pessimistic investor who believes that a particular security or market is headed downward.

Large Cap: Companies with a market capitalization value of approximately more than $10 billion. Market capitalization is calculated by multiplying the number of a company's shares outstanding by its stock price per share.

Mid Cap: A company with a market capitalization approximately between $2 and $10 billion.

Small Cap: A company with a market capitalization between approximately $500 million and $2 billion.

Growth Stock: Shares in a company whose earnings are expected to grow at an above-average rate relative to the market. A growth stock usually does not pay a dividend, as the company would prefer to reinvest retained earnings in capital projects.

Value Stock: A stock that tends to trade at a lower price relative to its fundamentals (i.e., dividends, earnings, sales, etc.). Some characteristics include a high-dividend yield, low price-to-book ratio (price divided by book value) and/or low price-to-earnings ratio.

Corporate Bond: A debt security issued by a corporation and sold to investors. The backing for the bond is usually the payment ability of the company, which is typically money to be earned from future operations.

"Junk" Bond: Also known as a "high-yield bond" or "speculative bond" that is rated "BB" or lower because of its high default risk. Typically, these bonds pay a higher interest rate to compensate the investor for the extra risk.

VIX - CBOE Volatility Index: Shows the market's expectation of 30-day volatility. It's constructed using the implied volatilities of a wide range of market options. VIX is a widely used measure of market risk and is often referred to as the "investor fear measure."

Short or Short Position: The sale of a borrowed security, commodity, or currency with the expectation that the asset will fall in value. The investor must eventually return the borrowed stock by buying it back from the open market. If the stock falls in price, the investor buys it for less than he or she sold it, making a profit.

Flight to Quality: The action of investors moving their capital away from riskier investments to safer investments. This flight is usually caused by uncertainty in the markets.

About the Author

Chip is a registered financial advisor and owner/partner at Coastal Wealth Management, LLC in Berlin, MD. He offers over 20 years of business and financial service experience, and currently holds FINRA Series 7 and 66 licenses, is licensed to sell Annuity and Life Insurance, along with earning the Chartered Retirement Planning Counselor (CRPC) designation.

Chip earned his Bachelor of Science degree from Widener University and his Master of Business Administration degree from Salisbury University.

A native of Ocean City, Maryland, when not spending time with his four sons and their lovely mother, Chip likes volunteering his time and going to the gym.

Made in the USA
Charleston, SC
05 February 2016